Chinese Takeout Cookbook

Favorite Chinese Takeout Recipes to Make at Home

Lina Chang

Copyrights

Disclaimer and Terms of Use

Effort has been made to ensure that the information in this book is accurate and complete. However, the author and the publisher do not warrant the accuracy of the information, text, and graphics contained within the book due to the rapidly changing nature of science, research, known and unknown facts, and internet. The author and the publisher do not hold any responsibility for errors, omissions, or contrary interpretation of the subject matter herein. This book is presented solely for motivational and informational purposes only.

The recipes provided in this book are for informational purposes only and are not intended to provide dietary advice. A medical practitioner should be consulted before making any changes in diet. Additionally, recipe cooking times may require adjustment depending on age and quality of appliances. Readers are strongly urged to take all precautions to ensure ingredients are fully cooked in order to avoid the dangers of foodborne illnesses. The recipes and suggestions provided in this book are solely the opinion of the author. The author and publisher do not take any responsibility for any consequences that may result due to following the instructions provided in this book.

ISBN: 978-1535150286

Printed in the United States

—— THE ——
COOK🍳BOOK
PUBLISHER

Contents

Introduction

Chinese takeout has been around for a long time. It's delicious, affordable, and conveniently available at any hour. It is served in the ingeniously designed and well-recognized cardboard box. Interestingly, most dishes on a takeout menu used to be considered strange by the Chinese themselves. The fortune cookie, for example, is an American invention. Other dishes that are now thought to be authentically Chinese, like fried rice and sweet-sour pork, are actually American.

A Little Bit of History

Most Chinese restaurants as we know them today serve food of Cantonese influence. The Cantonese traders and travelers are credited for bringing Chinese cuisine to the West. The first places that served Chinese food in the US were the "chow chows" of 19th century California that catered to the Cantonese laborers who built the transcontinental railways. Having been initially viewed with prejudice, the enterprising owners revised their recipes to suit American taste. This made some question its authenticity, though others began to appreciate its "Americanness." Chinese restaurants continued to evolve and gain American touches after WWII. Immigration laws became more accommodating and so other influences from Shanghai, Hunan, and Sichuan entered the country. By the '70s, fusion became popular and even Chinese restaurants in Asia began to adapt non-traditional ingredients in their recipes. The "chow chow" eateries of the 1800s have come a long way, with

Chinese restaurants today numbering even more than McDonald's outlets.

Ingredients

Chinese takeout recipes are somewhat removed from their authentic counterparts. Chinese cooks let nothing go to waste, and make use of exotic ingredients such as pig ears, chicken feet, and duck blood. Takeout has been modified to suit the conservative westerner's preference. In general, westernized Chinese food is looked upon as more fattening and lacking in spices.

Authentic Chinese dishes favor mostly vegetables, rice, and soybeans, while Chinese takeouts serve these more as side dishes. Many western ingredients like carrots, broccoli, onion, tomato, and dairy have been used to make Americanized recipes. Canned fruit such as pineapple and sweet caramelized sauces are actually "all-American." Takeouts offer limited seafood choices compared to the wide array of those found in ordinary Chinese cuisine. In spite of these differences, Chinese takeout is undeniably well loved and has made it full circle, finding acceptance even in the East.

Here are some ingredients you usually find in authentic as well as in Chinese takeout recipes.

Soy sauce
Light soy sauce, dark soy sauce, and regular soy sauce are all made from fermented soy beans. Light soy sauce is lighter in color though stronger in terms of saltiness. Dark soy sauce has been fermented for a longer duration. It is less salty, slightly sweet, and has a rich

caramel color. Regular soy sauce is somewhat in between light and dark sauces.

Cooking Oil

Deep frying is not really common in Chinese cooking but several oils are used. Peanut oil is used for its added fragrance. Corn and soy oil can also be used. Walnut oil is sought by pregnant women for its nourishing properties. Sesame oil is used to add flavor rather than for frying and is usually drizzled over dishes before serving.

Ginger, garlic and scallions (spring onion)

These are used fresh in various forms — whole, crushed, grated, or chopped. They are used for flavor and to remove "fishiness" as well as for their medicinal benefits.

Five-spice Powder

A combination of well-loved spices. It is made up of fennel, peppercorns, star anise, cinnamon, and cloves.

Rice Vinegar

This is what is traditionally used in Chinese recipes. It can be either white or black. It adds a distinct flavor to Asian dishes.

Oyster Sauce

A rich, thick, brown sauce made from oysters and soy sauce. It adds flavor to many dishes.

Cornstarch

Commonly mixed in water and used for thickening sauces. A slurry of cornstarch and water is usually added to simmering ingredients to arrive at just the right amount of sauce to coat the ingredients. It's also used to make crispy coatings for fried meats, vegetables, and seafood.

Salt
Salt is highly valued in Chinese cooking. It brings all flavors to life. (Which is why some doctors forbid Chinese food for patients who need to watch their sodium intake.)

Rice Wine
Called *Shaoxing*, rice wine is used in marinating and braising. Its flavor is somewhat similar to dry sherry. It is added by pouring around the rim of the wok when stir-frying for quicker dispersion of alcohol and better flavor. It is also mixed with soy sauce and spices for making sauces or marinades. Substitutes are dry sherry and sake. If you use *mirin,* add ½ a teaspoon of sugar for every tablespoon of mirin.

Cooking Methods

Chinese cuisine makes use of various techniques in cooking. Chinese chefs aim to preserve the freshness, color, nutrients, and texture of food. Takeout recipes make more use of frying. Although done in a wok, frying is not a popular cooking method in authentic Chinese cuisine. Breading is another method that has American roots. Americanized dishes, however, are evolving and westerners are becoming more adventurous in taste. Many Chinese restaurants are no longer hesitant to use traditional cooking methods and serve more authentic dishes.

Stir-Fry

This cooking method became popular in America because it is a quick, low-fat, and nutrient-preserving method of cooking. It involves cooking thinly sliced meat (sometimes pre-cooked) and vegetables with a soy sauce-based marinade. These are cooked in an ultra-hot wok with minimal oil and frequent stirring. The result is a hot, fresh dish of crisp and tasty ingredients. Large woks are preferred for better distribution of heat and more desirable texture and flavor. The key to stir-frying is to start with a very hot wok before adding oil.

Steaming

Chinese ingenuity and innovation is well-represented by this time, space, and fuel saving cooking method. The steamer is made up of bamboo baskets stacked one on top of the other, in about 3 layers. Several kinds of food can be cooked at a time over slow-boiling water. Popular steamed dishes are dim sum, such as buns or dumplings, pancakes, and fish.

Red Stewing

The name is taken from the resulting rich, brown color of the dishes using this cooking method. Unlike stir-fry, which uses the least amount of cooking time possible, this method requires several hours of cooking. Meats are usually seared first and cooked with soy sauce, rice wine, and traditional spices until tender and tasty.

Roasting

Large pieces of meat or whole chicken and duck are roasted in ovens. These are then chopped or sliced thinly and are usually served with a thick sauce or gravy.

Boiling

Commonly used for vegetables, which are boiled quickly, drained, and then served with a thick sauce. Noodles and soups are also cooked using this method.

Poaching

Fish are often cooked using this method. A tasty broth is used to impart flavor.

Deep frying

This method is said to be more popular in Americanized recipes, rather than in traditional cooking. The resulting dishes are crisp and tasty.

Tools for Chinese Takeout Recipes

The basic tools are more or less the same as those found in any regular kitchen. Here are some useful tools that will give your cooking a fun and authentic feel.

Wok

What is Chinese cooking without a wok? The wok is versatile and can be used for stir-frying, boiling, steaming, and deep-frying. Its rounded bottom results in more efficient use of heat. Chefs prefer large woks for more efficient heat distribution and better results in terms of texture and flavor.

Rice cooker

This is a very useful item for Chinese cooking. It does away with the need to constantly watch the rice cooking in a clay pot and gives you time to make other preparations. The rice cooker can also be used for boiling and steaming.

Steamer
The traditional steamer makes use of tiers of bamboo baskets but modern designs can be metal. This is used for dim sum and fish dishes.

Cleaver
A large knife used for cutting, slicing, and chopping. The flat side doubles as a smasher or crusher for garlic, ginger, and peppercorns.

Chopsticks
Chopsticks are indispensable to the Chinese cook. They can be used for picking up ingredients, loosening noodle strands, mixing, flipping, and even measuring powdered ingredients. The chopsticks for cooking are made of bamboo or wood and are longer than regular ones.

Chinese scissors
These make cutting much easier and faster than using knives. They can be used for meats, poultry, seafood, vegetables, and herbs.

Spider strainer
This tool is used for scooping and straining at the same time. It has a web-shaped mesh and is ideal for freshly-boiled noodles and deep fried rolls, chicken, or seafood.

Now that we've got the basic ingredients and tools together, it's time to start cooking!

Appetizer Recipes

Classic Egg Rolls

Serves: 8 - 10
Preparation Time: 10 minutes
Cooking Time: 15-29 minutes

Ingredients

For marinade

2 tablespoons soy sauce
2 tablespoons oyster sauce
1 teaspoon rice vinegar
3 cloves garlic, minced
2 teaspoons fresh ginger, minced
½ teaspoon brown sugar

For rolls

1 pound ground pork
1 tablespoon cornstarch

2 tablespoons vegetable oil
2 cups cabbage, shredded
1 medium carrot, peeled and shredded
Salt and pepper
1 package egg roll wrappers
Peanut oil for deep frying

Directions

1. Combine the ingredients for the marinade in a bowl, blending well.
2. Add the ground pork and cornstarch and combine. It's best to use your hands, clean or gloved, to do this.
3. Let the mixture marinade for about 5 minutes.
4. In a wok, heat the vegetable oil over medium heat. Stir-fry the pork until it is no longer pink.
5. Add the cabbage and carrots, and cook until heated through (about 2 minutes).
6. Season with salt and pepper as desired, and remove from the heat.
7. Place one wrapper at a time on a clean surface or tray, in a diamond shape.
8. Add about ¼ or ⅓ cup of the pork filling close to the tip of the diamond at the bottom, closest to you. Do not put too much filling or the wrapper will break while frying.
9. Fold the bottom tip of the wrapper over the filling. Roll tightly once.
10. Fold the left and right corners inward, and continue rolling up to the top corner.
11. Moisten the top corner with a little water or a paste of water and cornstarch to seal the roll.
12. Repeat until all the filling or wrappers are used up.

13. Prepare the peanut oil by heating it in a wok over medium-high heat. The oil is ready when wooden chopsticks immersed in the oil release tiny bubbles.
14. Working in batches, fry the rolls until they are golden brown. For more efficient heating and to get crisp rolls, do not overcrowd the rolls in the oil.
15. Use a spider strainer or tongs to lift the rolls out of the oil, and place them in a dish lined with paper towels.
16. Serve hot.

Fried Wontons

Serves: 10-12
Preparation Time: 1 ½ hours
Cooking Time: 20 minutes

Ingredients
1 pack (about 50 pieces) wonton wrappers
Oil for frying

<u>For the filling</u>
1 pound ground pork
2 tablespoons scallions, finely chopped
1 teaspoon sesame oil
1 tablespoon soy sauce
1 tablespoon rice wine
½ teaspoon sugar
1 tablespoon peanut oil
⅛ teaspoon ground white pepper

For the dipping sauce
1 tablespoon water
1 tablespoon sugar
1 ½ tablespoons light soy sauce
1 teaspoon Worcestershire sauce
½ teaspoon rice vinegar
1 teaspoon toasted sesame seeds

Directions
For the filling
1. Combine all the ingredients for the filling and mix thoroughly, with your hands or a food processor, until the mixture is paste-like in consistency.

To make the wontons
2. Line a baking sheet or tray with parchment paper.
3. Place a wrapper on a plate or clean surface, and put about a teaspoon of filling on the center.
4. Moisten the wrapper with a dab of water around the filling. This will help the sides of the wrapper to stick together.
5. Fold into either a rectangle or a triangle, pressing the edges together to seal. For rectangles, bring bottom corners together until they overlap, moisten with water, and press to seal. For triangles, bring the side corners together until they overlap and seal. Repeat until the filling is used up. Makes about 40-50 wontons.
6. Arrange the wontons on the lined baking sheet, leaving space to prevent sticking.
7. To store them, cover with plastic wrap and freeze. They keep for 2 months when frozen.

For dipping sauce
8. Prepare the sauce before frying the wontons, so the flavors can meld while the sauce is left standing.
9. Simply whisk the sauce ingredients together in a bowl.

To fry
10. Heat enough oil for frying in a wok or pan over medium heat. The oil should be 2 to 3 inches deep.
11. Fry the wontons in batches, turning over if needed, or keeping them submerged for even frying.
12. Let them drain on paper towels.
13. Serve with the dipping sauce.

Fried Spring Rolls

Serves: 25-50
Preparation Time: 30 minutes plus 20 minutes marinating time
Cooking Time: 30 minutes

Ingredients
2 pounds ground pork

For marinade
2 tablespoons cornstarch
2 tablespoons rice wine vinegar
2 tablespoons rice wine
1 teaspoon salt
1 teaspoon ground black pepper

For dipping sauce
2 tablespoons water
2 ½ teaspoons sugar
4 tablespoons hot sauce

6 tablespoons soy sauce
2 tablespoons rice vinegar
2 teaspoons rice wine

For filling
4 tablespoons vegetable oil, divided
10 cups cabbage, shredded
2 large carrots, shredded
3 cloves garlic, minced
1 teaspoon fresh ginger, peeled and grated
1 8-ounce can bamboo shoots, drained, squeezed, and shredded
10 dried shiitake mushrooms, rehydrated in boiling water, squeezed, and minced
1 cup green onion, chopped
2 tablespoons cornstarch
1 teaspoon sugar
4 tablespoons soy sauce
2 teaspoons sesame oil
2 tablespoons rice wine
50 spring roll wrappers
Oil for frying

Directions
For the pork
1.   In a large bowl, combine the ingredients for the marinade. Add the pork and mix well. Allow the mixture to marinate for 15-20 minutes.

For the dipping sauce
2.   In another bowl, whisk together the ingredients for the dipping sauce. Set it aside to allow the flavors to meld.

For the filling

3. Heat 2 tablespoons of oil in a wok over medium heat. Blanch the cabbage in the oil quickly, for about 2 minutes. Adjust the heat, if needed, to avoid scorching. Using a slotted spoon, remove the cabbage from the oil and set it aside to cool on a plate.

4. Using whatever oil is left in the wok (you may add another tablespoon, if needed), cook the carrots the same way. Remove the carrots from the oil using a slotted spoon and set them aside to cool.

5. Add the remaining oil to the wok and heat. Add the marinated pork and cook until the pork is browned and all the liquid is reduced.

6. Add the garlic and ginger and cook about 2-3 minutes longer. Do not burn the garlic.

7. Add the bamboo and mushrooms and heat through, about 3-5 minutes.

8. Remove the wok from the heat and set it aside to cool.

9. When the pork mixture has cooled down, add the cabbage and carrots, together with the mushrooms, green onion, cornstarch, sugar, soy sauce, sesame oil, and rice wine. Mix thoroughly.

To make the rolls

10. Place a wrapper on a clean surface. Position it so that it is diamond-shaped.

11. Place about ¼-⅓ cup of filling on the wrapper, about 1 ½ to 2 inches from the bottom corner.

12. Fold the bottom corner over the filling and roll snugly upwards once.

13. Fold in right and left corners and continue rolling up to top corner.

14. Moisten the top corner with water to help seal the roll. You may also use a paste of water and cornstarch as an adhesive to make it stick better.
15. Repeat until the filling is used up. You should be able to make about 50 rolls.
16. Heat the cooking or peanut oil in a wok or frying pan, about 2 inches deep, over medium heat.
17. Fry the rolls until they are golden brown. For efficient frying and crisp rolls, do not fry too many rolls at once; fry them in several batches.
18. Use a spider strainer to fish out the finished rolls, and place them on a dish lined with paper towels.
19. Serve while hot with the dipping sauce. The rolls may also be halved diagonally before serving.

Dumplings

Serves: 30-40
Preparation Time: 2 hours
Total Time: 2 hours, 15 minutes

Ingredients

3 pounds bok choy, washed
1 ½ pounds ground pork
⅔ cup rice wine
½ cup vegetable oil
3 tablespoons sesame oil
1 tablespoon salt
3 tablespoons soy sauce
¼ teaspoon white pepper
⅔ cup water
3-4 packages dumpling wrappers

Dipping sauce

½ cup soy sauce
½ tablespoon rice vinegar
1 dash hot chili sauce
1 green onion, sliced thinly

Directions

1. Cut the bottoms off the bok choy, and blanch it in boiling water. Transfer it immediately to ice cold water. Drain, squeeze the water out gently, and wipe it dry with paper towels. Chop the bok choy finely and place it in a large bowl.
2. Add the ground pork, rice wine, vegetable oil, sesame oil, salt, soy sauce, white pepper, and water, and mix thoroughly.
3. Line a baking sheet with parchment paper, and set it aside.
4. Place a wrapper on a clean surface and spoon about a tablespoon of filling into the center.
5. Moisten the edges with water and fold the circle over, in half.
6. Press the edges together to seal.
7. Fold the edges to get a fan-like shape (about 4 folds).

8. Arrange the dumplings on the baking sheet, not too close so they don't stick to each other.
9. To store, cover with cling wrap and freeze overnight. Transfer the frozen dumplings to another container or to Ziploc bags and replace in the freezer.
10. The dumplings may be boiled or fried. When boiled, cooked dumplings float to the top when ready. To fry, deep fry until golden brown or pan fry
11. Serve with a dipping sauce made of ½ cup of soy sauce, ½ tablespoon if rice vinegar, and a dash of chili sauce. Add green onions and mix well

Dumplings with Peanut Sauce

Serves: about 40 pieces
Preparation time: 1 hour 30 minutes
Cooking time: 30 minutes

Ingredients
Dumpling
1 pound ground pork
2 tablespoons soya sauce
1 teaspoon salt
1 tablespoon rice wine vinegar
¼ teaspoon white pepper
2 tablespoons sesame oil
2 tablespoons vegetable oil
3 green onions, sliced
1½ cups Napa cabbage, shredded
4 tablespoons bamboo shoots, shredded

22

1 teaspoon fresh ginger, grated
2 garlic cloves, minced
40-50 round dumpling wrappers
Egg wash for sealing (1 egg beaten with 1-2 tablespoons of water)
Peanut sauce
½ cup smooth organic peanut butter,
1 cup water
1 tablespoon soy sauce
1 tablespoon hoisin sauce
1 teaspoon chili paste
1 pinch hot chili pepper flakes
Crushed peanuts and sliced green onions for garnish

Directions
Dumpling
1. Warm 2 tablespoons of vegetable oil in a wok on medium-high heat. Add the garlic and ginger. Sauté for 30 seconds. Reduce heat to medium and add the green onions, Napa cabbage, and bamboo shoots. Sauté until the vegetables are tender. Remove from heat and let cool down for a few minutes.
2. Add the vegetable mixture to the raw ground pork. Mix well.
3. Place 1 teaspoon to 1½ teaspoon of the pork filling onto one half of the wrapper. Seal the dumpling by brushing lightly with some egg wash on the edges. Press lightly to seal. Pleat if desired.
4. You can cook the dumplings by either steaming (preferable for added flavors) or boiling them.
5. When boiling, add them to the pot only when the water has started boiling. Let them boil for about 12 minutes.

6. If you are using a bamboo steamer, place cabbage, bok choy or large lettuce leaves at the bottom of the steamer. It will prevent the dumplings from sticking to the bottom. Arrange the dumpling so they do not touch. Steam for 15 minutes.

Peanut Sauce

7. Combine sauce ingredients in a blender, mix until smooth.
8. Add some more water if necessary for the desired consistency.
9. Add enough sauce to the dumpling to coat well. Sprinkle with crushed peanuts and green onions if desired. Serve immediately

Note: this sauce can be very spicy depending on your chili paste. It is a good idea to taste to adjust the spice level. You can start by adding only a ¼ of the chili paste and omit the chili pepper flakes. Then adjust to own liking.

Shrimp Toast

Serves: 4
Preparation Time: 10 Minutes
Cooking Time: 5 Minutes

Ingredients

8 ounces shrimp, cooked and peeled
2 cloves garlic, crushed
1 tablespoon soy sauce
1 teaspoon sesame oil
1 large egg
4 slices white bread, crusts removed
1 tablespoon sesame seeds, toasted
2 tablespoons vegetable oil
Sweet and sour sauce, to use as dip

Directions

1. Use a blender or food processor to puree the shrimp and garlic.
2. Add the soy sauce, sesame oil, and egg. Pulse or process a little longer until paste-like in consistency.
3. Spread the paste on the bread slices.
4. Sprinkle with sesame seeds. Press down on the sesame seeds with a spatula or the back of a spoon so they stick to the paste.
5. Heat the oil in a skillet over medium heat.
6. Cut the bread into small triangles, and fry them with the spread side up until golden brown, about 3-4 minutes.
7. Drain on a cooling rack or a plate lined with paper towels.
8. Serve with sweet and sour sauce.

Garlic Spare Ribs

Serves: 4-6
Preparation Time: 15 minutes
Cooking Time: 45 minutes

Ingredients
Water for boiling ribs
4 pounds spareribs, cut apart

For sauce
1 ½ cups brown sugar
1 ½ cups water
5 garlic cloves
3 ½ tablespoons light soy sauce
1 tablespoon oyster sauce
1 ½ tablespoons dry mustard
Spring onions, chopped (for garnish)

Directions

1. Fill a pot with water and bring it to a boil.
2. Add the spareribs, cover, and simmer until the meat is tender (about 30 minutes).
3. Remove the ribs from the broth and drain.
4. In another pot or wok, combine the ingredients for the sauce.
5. Bring it to a gentle boil, and add the spareribs.
6. Bring once again to a boil, and simmer for 10-15 minutes.
7. Serve garnished with chopped spring onion, if desired.

Soup Recipes

Egg Drop Soup

Serves 4
Preparation Time: 10 Minutes
Cooking Time: 5 Minutes

Ingredients
<u>For thickener</u>
2 tablespoons corn starch
3 tablespoons water

For soup

1 14-ounce can chicken broth
1 cup water
½ tomato, diced
¼ teaspoon white pepper
½ teaspoon salt
2 large eggs, lightly beaten
1 stalk spring onion, chopped

Directions

1. Prepare the thickener by combining the water and cornstarch. Stir it into a slurry, and set it aside.
2. In a saucepan, bring the broth and water to a boil.
3. Add the tomato, pepper, salt, and thickener. Stir until the soup begins to thicken, and remove it from the heat.
4. Pour in the beaten egg and stir it a couple of times with a pair of chopsticks to form egg "ribbons".
5. Cover, and cook 2 minutes longer.
6. Sprinkle with spring onion and serve immediately.

Hot and Sour Soup

Serves: 10-12
Preparation Time: 5 minutes
Cooking Time: 25 minutes

Ingredients
<u>For thickener</u>
5 tablespoons cornstarch
5 tablespoons water

<u>For soup</u>
6 cups chicken broth
4 ounces chicken breast, sliced thinly
2 tablespoons soy sauce

½ cup dried shiitake mushrooms, soaked in hot water to rehydrate, de-stemmed and sliced
1 15-ounce can peeled straw mushrooms
2 tablespoons garlic red chili paste
¾ teaspoon ground pepper
½ ounce dried black fungus (soak in water for an hour before using)
1 7-ounce can sliced bamboo shoots
1 7-ounce can sliced water chestnuts
1 15-ounce can baby sweet corn cobs
½ pound soft tofu, sliced into ¼-inch cubes
¼ cup rice vinegar
4 eggs, beaten
1 teaspoon sesame oil
Green onion, finely chopped (to garnish)

Directions

1. Mix the cornstarch and water together. Stir to make a slurry, and set it aside.
2. In a pot, bring the broth to a boil, and reduce to a simmer.
3. Add the chicken, soy sauce, mushrooms, and chili paste. Simmer for 10 minutes.
4. Add pepper, fungus, bamboo shoots, water chestnuts, baby corn, and tofu. Simmer for another 10 minutes.
5. Add the thickener while stirring. Stir until the soup begins to thicken.
6. Pour in eggs in a thin stream, stirring constantly. Cook for about 10 seconds and then remove from the heat.
7. Stir in the sesame oil.
8. Serve garnished with chopped green onion.

Wonton Soup

Serves: 4-6
Preparation Time: 2 hours
Cooking Time: 30 minutes

Ingredients
1 package wonton wrappers

For wonton filling
½ pound medium prawns (shelled, deveined)
½ pound ground pork
1 tablespoon shallots, finely chopped
¼ cup cilantro, finely chopped
2 green onion stalks, thinly sliced
1 teaspoon fish sauce
1 teaspoon sugar
2 teaspoon rice wine

For broth
1 cinnamon stick
1 tablespoon fennel
1 tablespoon coriander seeds
1 star anise
6 cups chicken broth
2 tablespoons fish sauce
1 tsp white sugar
½ cup cilantro leaves, for garnish
Green onion, for garnish
Chili sauce

Directions
1. Wipe the prawns dry with paper towels, and chop finely.
2. Combine the ingredients for the filling in a bowl, and mix thoroughly.
3. Place a wonton wrapper on a clean surface.
4. Place about 1 teaspoon of filling in the middle of the wrapper. Moisten the wrapper with a dab of water around the filling; this will help the sides of the wrapper to stick together.

5. Fold into either a rectangle or a triangle, pressing the edges together to seal. For rectangles, bring the bottom corners together until they overlap, moisten with water, and press to seal. For triangles, bring side corners together until they overlap, and seal. Repeat until filling is used up.
6. Place the wontons on a parchment lined baking sheet. Leave some space between pieces to prevent sticking. For long term storage (about 2 months), cover with plastic wrap and freeze.
7. In a pot, bring water to a boil. Drop in the wontons in batches, and stir with chopsticks to prevent them from sticking to pan. The wontons are done when they float up to the surface, after about 3 minutes.
8. Distribute the wontons into serving bowls.
9. Place the cinnamon stick, fennel, coriander, and star anise in a square piece of cheesecloth, and tie it into a knot.
10. To prepare the soup, bring the chicken broth to a boil. Immerse the spice pouch in the boiling broth. Cover the pot and reduce it to a simmer.
11. Simmer for 30 minutes, and remove the spice pouch.
12. Add the fish sauce and sugar, adjusting the amounts according to your taste.
13. Scoop the hot broth into the bowls ready with wontons.
14. Serve garnished with cilantro and green onions, with chili sauce on the side.

Noodle Recipes and Rice Recipes

Singapore Noodles

Serves: 2
Preparation Time: 20 minutes
Cooking Time: 10 minutes

Ingredients
2 eggs, beaten
1 14-ounce pack rice stick noodles
8-12 shrimps, peeled and deveined
1 tablespoon vegetable oil
1 Chinese sausage, chopped
3 cups napa cabbage, shredded
½ red onion, sliced thinly
3 dried red chili peppers
1 carrot, julienned

1 ½ tablespoons curry powder
2 teaspoons salt
1 tablespoon rice wine
½ teaspoon sesame oil
½ tablespoon soy sauce
Pinch of white pepper
1 green onion, chopped

Directions
1. Cook the eggs into an omelet. Cut them into strips, and set them aside.
2. Soak the noodles in cold water for 20 minutes. Drain them when you are just about to cook.
3. Dry the shrimps with paper towels and make slits lengthwise, or "butterfly" them.
4. Heat the oil in the wok over high heat. Stir-fry the shrimps and sausage until the shrimps turn orange, about 10 seconds.
5. Add the cabbage, onion, chilies, and carrot. Continue stir-frying for about 30 seconds.
6. Add the curry powder and stir.
7. Maintain the heat at high. Tear the drained noodles into about 8-inch long strands while adding them to the wok.
8. Add the salt and wine. Mix continuously, and scrape to prevent the noodles from sticking to the bottom of the wok.
9. When the noodles have turned yellowish from the curry, add the sesame oil, soy sauce, and white pepper. Mix 2 minutes longer.
10. Top with the omelet strips and sprinkle with green onion.
11. Serve while hot.

Beef Chow Fun

Serves: 2-3
Preparation Time: 1 hour
Cooking Time: 5 minutes

Ingredients
8 ounces flank steak, cut across the grain in strips

For the marinade
¼ teaspoon baking soda
1 teaspoon corn starch
1 teaspoon soy sauce
1 teaspoon oil

For the rest of the dish
3 tablespoons oil, divided
1 thumb ginger, cut into thin slices
4 scallions, halved lengthwise and cut into 3-inch pieces

1 12-ounce pack fresh flat rice noodles, pre-cut
2 tablespoons rice wine
½ teaspoon sesame oil
2 tablespoons dark soy sauce
2 tablespoons regular soy sauce
⅛ teaspoon sugar
Salt and white pepper, to taste
4 ounces fresh mung bean sprouts

Directions

1. Mix the ingredients for the marinade together, and marinate the beef for 1 hour.
2. Heat the wok to smoking. Add 1 ½ teaspoons of oil, and sear the beef until browned. Remove the beef from wok and set it aside.
3. Add the rest of the oil and cook the ginger until fragrant.
4. Add the scallions and noodles, spreading them evenly inside the wok.
5. Stir-fry over high heat for about 15 seconds.
6. Add the wine, spooning it around the rim of the wok.
7. Add the sesame oil, soy sauces, sugar and white pepper. Scrape the bottom of the wok with a spatula, and lift the noodles upwards to mix.
8. Keep the heat high, and continue mixing the noodles until they are evenly coated with sauce, and heated through.
9. Add the beef and sprouts, mix, and cook until the sprouts tender and the beef is heated through.

Pork Chow Mein

Serves: 1
Preparation Time: 5 minutes
Cooking Time: 20 minutes

Ingredients:
For marinade
1 teaspoon rice wine
1 teaspoon soy sauce
Dash salt

For noodles
4 ounces lean pork, cut into thin strips
7 ounces Hong Kong noodles (chow mein noodles)
1 teaspoon vegetable oil, for noodles, divided
1 tablespoon peanut or vegetable oil, for stir-frying
Dash ground chili
½ small onion, minced
1 teaspoon ginger, chopped
1 tablespoon green onion, chopped
½ cup cabbage, shredded

1 small carrot, julienned
½ cup green beans, sliced
2 small red bell peppers, sliced into strips
½ teaspoon salt
2 tablespoons chicken stock
1-2 tablespoons tomato ketchup (or according to taste)

Directions

1. Mix the ingredients for the marinade together. Stir in the pork, and let it stand for 5-10 minutes.

To cook the noodles

2. Prepare the steamer by filling it with water up to ¼ full, and bringing it to a gentle boil. Coat the bottom of the steamer basket with oil to prevent sticking.
3. Steam the noodles for 2-3 minutes.
4. Transfer the noodles to a bowl, and stir in ½ a teaspoon of oil with chopsticks.
5. Put the noodles back into the steaming basket and steam for another 2-3 minutes.
6. Transfer them to a bowl, and set aside.

To cook the chow mein

7. Heat a wok over high heat. Add the peanut or vegetable oil and stir-fry the pork until it is no longer pink in color.
8. Add ground chili, onion, ginger, and green onion. Stir-fry until fragrant.
9. Add the cabbage, carrot, green beans, and bell pepper, and cook for 1 minute, stirring constantly.
10. Add the salt and chicken stock, and cook until the stock dries up.
11. Add the ketchup and noodles. Mix until well-blended and heated through.

Chicken, Pork, and Shrimp Lo Mein

Serves: 4
Preparation Time: 30 Minutes
Cooking Time: 20 Minutes

Ingredients

2 cups chicken broth, divided
¼ cup rice wine
¼ cup soy sauce
4 teaspoons cornstarch
4 ounces lean pork, very finely sliced
4 ounces boneless skinless chicken breasts, cut into thin slices
2 teaspoons sesame oil
2-4 pieces shrimp, cleaned, shelled and deveined
3 cloves garlic, minced
½ teaspoon ground ginger

4 green onions, chopped, plus more for garnish
½ can water chestnuts, chopped
2 cups cabbage, finely shredded
1 cup celery, thinly sliced
1 cup frozen green peas, thawed and drained
1 carrot, peeled and shredded
8 ounces thin or angel hair spaghetti, cooked and drained

Directions
1. Pour a ½ cup of broth into a skillet.
2. In a separate bowl, add the wine, soy sauce, and cornstarch to the remaining broth. Stir well, and set aside.
3. Bring the broth in the skillet to a boil. Add the pork and boil it for 2 minutes. Add the chicken and cook until both are no longer pink in the center.
4. Use a slotted spoon to remove the pork and chicken to a plate, and set it aside. Discard any liquid left in the skillet.
5. Heat the sesame oil in the skillet, and keep the heat at medium-high.
6. Cook the shrimp, garlic, and ginger until they are fragrant and the shrimp has become orange in color.
7. Add the green onion, water chestnuts, cabbage, celery, peas, and carrots, and cook for 3 minutes or until tender-crisp.
8. Add the meat and pre-cooked pasta, and toss for about 2 minutes.
9. Stir the cornstarch mixture and pour it over the pasta.
10. Cook, while stirring, until thickened, and remove it from the heat.
11. Garnish with chopped green onion, if desired.

Fried Rice

Serves: 2-4
Preparation Time: 15 minutes
Cooking Time: 10 minutes

Ingredients
2 tablespoons vegetable oil
1 medium onion, chopped
4 cloves garlic, minced
1 teaspoon ginger, minced
⅓ cup boneless chicken, diced
⅓ cup Chinese sausage or ham, chopped
Salt and pepper
½ cup frozen peas
½ cup carrot, cut into small cubes
Water, if needed
1 tablespoon sesame oil
2 tablespoons soy sauce

½ teaspoon sugar (optional)
¼ cup green onions, thinly sliced
2 cups cooked day-old rice
1 egg, fried (optional)
Garlic chili sauce

Directions

1. Heat the vegetable oil in a wok over medium-high heat.
2. Add the onion, garlic, and ginger. Stir for 30 seconds to 1 minute or until fragrant.
3. Add the chicken and cook until it is no longer pink, then stir in Chinese sausage or ham, and season with salt and pepper.
4. Add the carrot and cook until tender. Add water, 1 tablespoon at a time, if more moisture is needed to cook the carrots.
5. Add the sesame oil, soy sauce, and sugar, if using.
6. Add the rice and mix well. Scrape the bottom of the wok with a spatula and lift the rice upwards to mix thoroughly.
7. Add the frozen peas.
8. Cook for about 10 minutes, mixing frequently.
9. Add the green onion and mix well. Adjust the flavor with seasonings, as desired.
10. Place on serving dish topped with a fried egg (optional), and with garlic chili sauce on the side.

Yang Chow Fried Rice

Servings: 4
Preparation Time: 30 minutes
Cooking Time: 10 minutes

Ingredients
2 large eggs, scrambled (cooked)
2-3 tablespoons vegetable or peanut oil
1 medium onion, minced
½ cup ham, cut into cubes
½ cup Chinese roast pork
5 cups cooked or day-old rice, lumps broken
¾ cup frozen peas, thawed
4 ounces fresh shrimp, shelled and deveined

1 ½ teaspoons salt
¼ teaspoon sugar
1 teaspoon rice wine
2 green onions, finely chopped
2 cups lettuce, finely chopped
⅛ teaspoon freshly ground white pepper

Directions

1. Break the scrambled eggs into small pieces and set them aside.
2. In a saucepan, boil some water to blanch the shrimps. Immerse the shrimps momentarily, until the color changes to orange. Remove them from pot, drain them, and set them aside.
3. Heat a wok over high heat. Add the oil and stir in the onion. Cook until it is translucent.
4. Add the ham and pork, and cook for 30 seconds to heat through.
5. Add the rice, and mix for 2 minutes to heat it through. Use the spatula to remove any remaining lumps, sprinkling water over any stubborn ones to soften them.
6. Add the shrimps and peas and cook, stirring constantly, for 2 minutes more.
7. Stir in the salt and sugar, and drizzle the wine around the rim of the wok.
8. Continue mixing, scraping the bottom of the wok with the spatula and lifting the rice upwards. Sprinkle with water to moisten or add a little more oil, if needed.
9. Add the scrambled eggs, green onion, lettuce, and pepper, and mix until the lettuce is wilted.

Pork Recipes

Twice Cooked Pork

Serves: 4
Preparation Time: 10 minutes
Cooking Time: 35 minutes

Ingredients
2 quarts water
1 pound slab of pork belly
2 slices ginger
2 tablespoons oil, divided
1 ½ tablespoons spicy broad bean paste
2 cloves garlic, sliced
2 long hot green peppers, seeds removed and cut into 1 ½-inch pieces
1 medium leek, split lengthwise, washed thoroughly, and cut in 2-inch pieces
1 tablespoon rice wine
1 teaspoon soy sauce

¼ teaspoon sugar

Directions
1. Fill a pot with 2 quarts of water and bring it to a boil.
2. Place the slab of pork belly and ginger in the boiling water. Bring to a boil again.
3. Reduce the heat and simmer for 30 minutes, or until the pork is tender and cooked through.
4. Take the pork out of the pot and place it under cold running water for 1 minute, then put it on a cooling rack to drain and set it aside.
5. Assemble all the other ingredients before beginning the next step or else pork will dry out.
6. Slice the pork into ⅛-inch slices.
7. Heat a wok over high heat. Add 1 tablespoon of oil and swirl it around.
8. Sear the pork slices until lightly caramelized, about 1 or 2 minutes. Reduce the heat to medium-low.
9. Remove the pork from the wok and set it aside.
10. Heat the remaining oil and add the bean paste. Let it fry until it is fragrant, about 30 seconds. Be careful not to scorch the bean paste; it should be red in color.
11. Add the garlic. Turn the heat up and return the pork to wok.
12. Stir in the peppers, leeks, wine, and sugar. The dish is ready when the leeks are wilted.

Moo Shu Pork

Serves: 4
Preparation Time: 45 Minutes
Cooking Time: 15 Minutes

Ingredients
<u>For pancakes</u>
2 cups flour, unsifted
¾ cup water
Sesame oil

<u>For filling</u>
3 eggs, scrambled (cooked)
3 tablespoons canola oil
1 pound pork, julienned
1 tablespoon garlic, minced
1 tablespoon ginger, minced
2 cups white cabbage, shredded

51

¾ cup bamboo shoots, rinsed well, drained and julienned
½ red bell pepper, trimmed and finely julienned
¾ cup wood ear mushrooms, soaked in water overnight (refrigerated) to rehydrate, sliced
1 cup shiitake mushrooms, sliced
10 dried lily buds, soaked in water overnight (refrigerated) to rehydrate
1 cup hoisin sauce
1-2 tablespoons rice wine
1 bunch green onion or scallions, leaves slit several times to make a scallion brush
Salt and pepper

Directions
For the pancakes
1. Boil the water.
2. Place the flour in a bowl and make a well in the center.
3. Add the hot water and mix. You may gradually add more flour to get a kneadable dough.
4. Knead the dough on a floured surface for 5 minutes, then cover and let it rest for 30 minutes.
5. Knead it again for 5 minutes, and roll it into a 1 ½-inch cylinder.
6. Divide the cylinder into 16 pieces, and roll each piece into a smooth ball.
7. Spread some sesame oil on your hands and flatten a ball of dough.
8. Roll it into a smooth disc, and brush the top with sesame oil. Make another disc of a similar size and place on top of first disc. Roll them out into a 6- to7-inch diameter double disc. Repeat for the rest of the dough balls.

9. Heat a skillet until water sprinkled into it bounces about in a small balls. Brush on a thin coat of sesame oil. Cook the double pancakes for 30 seconds on each side, without any browning. Remove them from the pan and slap them on a hard surface to separate the 2 discs. Peel away the 2 discs from each other, and place them on a sheet of foil. Repeat this procedure for the rest of the discs.
10. To steam the pancakes, form a packet by sealing foil over the discs. Place the foil packet in a steamer or double boiler and steam it for 20-30 minutes.
11. Serve hot.

For filling
12. Heat a wok over high heat. Add the oil and cook the pork for only 1 minute before removing it from the wok. Place it on a dish lined with paper towels, and set it aside.
13. Add the garlic, ginger, and ear mushrooms to the wok and stir-fry them for 2-3 minutes. Season with salt and pepper.
14. Add the cabbage, bamboo shoots, red bell pepper, remaining mushrooms and lily buds. Cook 3-4 minutes longer.
15. Add half of the hoisin sauce and the wine. Adjust the flavor with salt and pepper, according to taste.

To assemble
16. Lay a hot pancake or tortilla on a clean surface and use the scallion brush to spread some hoisin sauce on it.

17. Add a spoonful of the pork mixture. Top with a little more hoisin sauce, and roll it up.
18. Repeat until all the pancakes are used, and serve hot.

Shanghai Pork Chops

Serves: 4
Preparation Time: 5 minutes with 2 hours marinating time
Cooking Time: 10 minutes

Ingredients
4 pork chops

For marinade
½ cup light brown sugar
½ cup soy sauce
¼ cup ketchup
3 green onions, thinly sliced
1 teaspoon fresh ginger, peeled and grated
1 teaspoon garlic, minced

Directions

1. Combine the ingredients for the marinade. Place it in a shallow container with a lid, or in a resealable bag.
2. Put the pork chops in the marinade, and turn to coat. Seal the container and refrigerate it for at least 2 hours.
3. Grill the pork chops for 8-10 minutes on each side, on a preheated grill over medium-high heat.

Chinese Roasted Ribs

Serves: 6
Preparation Time: 20 minutes
Cooking Time: 1 hour, 30 minutes

Ingredients
1 large rack ribs

For marinade
5 cloves garlic, minced
1 tablespoon pineapple, minced
2 tablespoons pineapple juice
1 tablespoon freshly-squeezed lime juice
1 tablespoon salt

⅓ cup sugar

1 tablespoon honey

2 tablespoons peanut oil

2 tablespoons hoisin sauce

1 teaspoon ground bean sauce

1 tablespoon tomato paste

1 tablespoon water

⅓ cup ketchup

½ tablespoon 5-spice powder

1 teaspoon fresh ground pepper

½ tablespoon paprika

1 star anise, ground

Directions

1. Mix all the ingredients for the marinade together in a bowl.
2. Brush the marinade over the ribs. Cover them with foil or plastic wrap and marinate overnight in the refrigerator.
3. Preheat oven to 325°F, and line roasting a pan with foil. Add water up to ½-inch deep.
4. Place the roasting rack in the pan, and position the ribs, rib-side up, on it.
5. Roast for 30 minutes, then turn the ribs over and roast 60 minutes longer. Replenish water in pan, if needed, so the ribs don't become too dry.
6. Broil for a few minutes for a darker color, if desired.

Sweet and Sour Pork

Serves: 2

Preparation Time: 10 minutes plus 30 minutes marinating time

Cooking Time: 20 minutes

Ingredients

8 ounces boneless pork shoulder, cut into bite-size pieces

Sauce
⅛ teaspoon salt
1 tablespoon sugar
2 teaspoons rice wine
2 teaspoons rice vinegar
1 tablespoon soy sauce
2 tablespoon plum sauce
¾ teaspoon cornstarch
¼ cup water

For marinade
2 teaspoons rice wine
½ teaspoon oyster sauce
½ teaspoon regular soy sauce

Other ingredients
1 egg
Cooking oil for deep-frying plus 2 teaspoons for sautéing
1 teaspoon plus about ⅓ cup cornstarch
1 onion, sliced
1 thumb ginger, peeled and minced
½ cup pineapple cubes
2 bell peppers, cut into 1-inch pieces
1 small ripe tomato, cut into wedges
1 green onion, thinly sliced
Cooked rice, for serving

Directions

1. Combine the sauce ingredients in a bowl and set it aside.
2. Mix together the ingredients for the marinade. Stir in the pork and marinate for 30 minutes.
3. Beat the egg in a medium-sized bowl, and put the cornstarch on a plate.
4. After marinating, dip the pork pieces in the beaten egg, and then into the cornstarch. Coat the pork well, and allow it to set for 3 minutes.
5. Heat a wok and add oil to about ¾-inch deep. Heat the oil to about 350°F.
6. Fry the pork in batches for 2-3 minutes, and place them on a dish lined with paper towels. After all the pieces have been pre-fried, heat up the wok further to 375°F. Drop all the pork in to refry, until it is brown and crisp.

7. Heat a clean wok over high heat. Add 2 teaspoons of oil, and the onion, ginger and pineapple. Cook for 2 minutes, until the pineapple begins to caramelize a little. Add the bell pepper and cook, stirring, until tender-crisp.
8. Stir in the sauce mixture and the tomato. Cook until it begins to boil and thicken.
9. Stir in the pork and mix to coat well. Remove the wok from the heat.
10. Sprinkle with green onion and serve with rice.

Beef Recipes

Beef with Garlic Sauce

Serves: 2
Preparation Time: 10 minutes plus 30 minutes marinating time
Cooking Time: 20 minutes

Ingredients
12 ounces beef tenderloin, thinly sliced
¼ cup oil for frying

For marinade
¼ teaspoon salt
¼ teaspoon sugar
½ teaspoon white pepper
1 tablespoon soy sauce
1 teaspoon vinegar

For sauce
1 ½ teaspoons cornstarch
1 tablespoon water

2 tablespoons rice vinegar
2 tablespoons granulated sugar
1 tablespoon light soy sauce
1 tablespoon dark soy sauce
2 teaspoons Chinese rice wine or dry sherry
½ teaspoon chili sauce
¼ teaspoon sesame oil
4 garlic cloves, chopped
1 medium white onion, chopped
½ cup green onions, sliced
10 water chestnuts, sliced
Chicken stock or water, as needed

Directions
1. Combine the ingredients for the marinade, and marinate the beef strips for 30 minutes.
2. In a small bowl, combine the water and cornstarch. Set it aside.
3. In a separate bowl, combine the vinegar, sugar, soy sauces, wine, chili sauce and sesame oil.
4. When the beef is ready, heat the oil for frying in a wok over high heat. Fry the beef until it is tender, and remove it to a paper-lined plate. Set it aside.
5. Remove any oil in excess of 2 tablespoons from the wok. Stir in the garlic until fragrant. Add the onions, green onions, and water chestnuts, and fry for 2-3 minutes. Stir the vinegar and wine mixture, and add it to the wok. Add broth or water, one tablespoon at a time, if needed to prevent the sauce from drying up. Simmer for about 3 minutes.
6. Add the pre-fried beef to the wok.

7. Stir the cornstarch in water, and pour it into the wok. Cook, with stirring, until the mixture thickens and coats the beef. Adjust the taste with seasonings, as needed.
8. Serve with rice.

Ginger Beef

Serves: 2-3
Preparation Time: 30 minutes
Cooking Time: 15 minutes

Ingredients
1 pound flank steak, sliced thinly

For marinade
2 tablespoons dark soy sauce
1 tablespoon rice wine
1 teaspoon sugar
1 tablespoon minced

For sauce
1 tablespoon rice wine
1 tablespoon light soy sauce
2 tablespoons rice vinegar
2 tablespoons sugar
2 tablespoons water

Hot chili oil or crushed red pepper flakes, to taste

For batter
¼ cup flour
¼ cup cornstarch
1 tablespoon vegetable oil
1 tablespoon hot chili oil (optional)
⅓ cup water, or as needed

Other ingredients
4 to 5 cups oil for deep frying
2 tablespoons oil for stir-frying, or as needed
3 red chili peppers, seeds left in, chopped
2 cloves garlic, minced
1 tablespoon fresh ginger, minced
1 small carrot, julienned
1 stalk celery, cut into thin strips
1 red bell pepper, julienned
1 teaspoon sesame oil

Directions

1. Combine the ingredients for the marinade, and marinate the beef for 30 minutes.
2. Mix together the sauce ingredients in a small bowl, and set it aside.
3. Prepare all the ingredients.
4. Begin to make the batter by combining the flour and cornstarch. Make a well in the center, and add the oil and chili oil (optional). Mix, while adding the water gradually. Use just enough water to reach the right consistency. The batter is just right when it lightly drips off the back of a wooden spoon.
5. Dip the marinated beef into the batter.

6. Preheat the wok over high heat. Add the oil for frying and heat to 350°F.
7. Deep fry the beef until it is golden brown. Lift it out of the oil, and transfer it to a plate lined with paper towels.
8. Heat the oil up to 400°F.
9. Fry the beef again until crispy, and remove it from the wok.
10. Heat a clean wok over high heat and add the oil for stir-frying. Add the chilies, minced garlic and ginger. Sauté until fragrant and chilies begin to blister.
11. Add the carrot and cook for about 1 minute.
12. Add the celery and bell pepper. Stir-fry for about 30 seconds.
13. Push the vegetables to the sides of the wok and pour in the sauce mixture.
14. Bring it to a boil (check that vegetables don't get scorched) and add the fried beef.
15. Mix all ingredients together and cook to heat through.
16. Remove from heat, stir in the sesame oil, and serve.

Szechuan Beef Recipe

Serves: 2
Preparation Time: 20 minutes
Cooking Time: 5 minutes

Ingredients
8 ounces beef tenderloin, cut into strips

<u>Marinade</u>
1 teaspoon cornstarch
½ teaspoon rice wine
1 teaspoon dark soy sauce

Sauce

½ tablespoon oyster sauce
½ tablespoon chili garlic sauce
1 ½ teaspoons soy sauce
2 teaspoons sugar
2 tablespoons water
½ teaspoon chili oil
½ teaspoon sesame oil

Other ingredients

2 tablespoons oil, divided
2 cloves garlic, minced
¼ small green bell pepper, julienned
¼ small red bell pepper, julienned
1 small carrot, julienned
½ teaspoon chili oil or according to taste
2 stalks green onion, cut into strips

Directions

1. Combine the ingredients for the marinade. Stir in the beef, and marinate for 15-30 minutes.
2. In a bowl, mix together the sauce ingredients, and set aside.
3. Heat a wok over high heat. Add 1 tablespoon of oil and sear the beef until partly browned. Transfer it to a paper-lined plate.
4. Scrape off any brown bits from the wok, and add the remaining oil.
5. Add garlic and stir-fry until fragrant.
6. Stir in the peppers and carrot. Cook for about 30 seconds, and add the beef back to the wok.
7. Pour in the sauce mixture and stir well.
8. Add the green onion and chili oil. Stir for 30 seconds, or until the sauce is of the desired thickness.
9. Serve.

Beef Chop Suey

Serves: 2
Preparation Time: 5 minutes plus 1 hour marinating time
Cooking Time: 15-20 minutes

Ingredients

Marinade

1 tablespoon rice wine
2 teaspoons oyster sauce
1 teaspoon cornstarch
White pepper

Slurry/Thickener

¾ cups chicken stock

1 teaspoon cornstarch

2-3 tablespoons peanut oil, as needed

½ pound skirt steak, cut into strips

2 cloves garlic, minced

½ stalk celery, diced

½ onion, minced

½ carrot, shredded

3 button mushrooms, sliced

½ cup broccoli florets

10 snow peas, trimmed,

1 ½ teaspoons sesame oil

Rice or noodles for serving

Directions

1. Combine the ingredients for the marinade. Marinate the beef for 1 hour.
2. Mix the ingredients for the thickener in a small bowl, and set aside.
3. Heat a wok over high heat. Add the peanut or vegetable oil, and sauté the garlic until fragrant.
4. Add the meat and fry until tender and no longer pink in color. Transfer it to a plate, and set it aside.
5. Stir-fry the garlic, celery, onion, carrot, and mushrooms until tender-crisp.
6. Add the cabbage, snow peas, and beef.
7. Stir the thickener and add it to the wok. Stir, and bring it to a simmer, until the sauce has thickened. Season with sesame oil.
8. Serve with rice or noodles.

Beef in Oyster Sauce

Serves: 2-4

Preparation Time: 5 minutes plus 30 minutes marinating time

Cooking Time: 12 minutes

Ingredients
1 pound beef tenderloin, thinly sliced

For marinade
2 tablespoons oyster sauce
1 tablespoon soy sauce
1 teaspoon salt
½ teaspoon ground black pepper

Other ingredients
1 tablespoon ginger, minced
1 tablespoon garlic, minced

2 teaspoons chili, minced (optional)
2 cups fresh spinach, cleaned
3 tablespoons cooking oil

Directions

1. Combine the ingredients for the marinade, and marinate the beef for 30 minutes.
2. Heat a wok over high heat and add the cooking oil.
3. Stir-fry the ginger, garlic, and chili until fragrant.
4. Add the spinach, and stir-fry until wilted.
5. Remove the vegetables from the wok, leaving as much oil as possible, and set them aside in a serving dish.
6. Use the remaining oil in the wok to fry the marinated beef until cooked and browned.
7. Arrange the cooked beef over the spinach mixture.

Chinese Pepper Steak

Serves: 4-6
Preparation Time: 10 minutes
Marinating Time: 2-4 hours
Cook Time: 15 minutes

Ingredients
1 pound flank steak, sliced very thinly against the grain
5 garlic cloves, minced
1 tablespoon ginger, minced
4 tablespoons soy sauce
1 tablespoon coarse ground black pepper
½ cup sherry
½ to 1 teaspoon crushed dry chilies, more if you want it very spicy
1 tablespoon corn starch
1 large yellow onion, sliced
2 green bell pepper, sliced

½ teaspoon salt
4 tablespoons peanut oil
Rice for serving

Directions

1. In a large bowl, add soy sauce, sherry, ginger, garlic, black pepper, chilies, and corn starch. Whisk until all ingredients are incorporated. Add steak, toss until coated and refrigerate for 2-4 hours.
2. In a hot pan or wok, heat three tablespoons of peanut oil on high heat. Quickly brown the steak. Stir frying the steak for no longer than 20 seconds. Remove steak and set aside.
3. Add more oil if needed and add bell peppers, onion and salt. Stir fry for 3 to 4 minutes or just until peppers are tender.
4. Add steak back in and add the remaining marinade. Reduce heat and simmer till sauce has thickened.
5. Serve over your choice of rice.

Beef & Broccoli

Serves: 4
Prep time: 10 minutes
Cooking Time: 20 minutes

Ingredients
1 pound beef, sliced into thin strips
2-3 tablespoons cooking or peanut oil
3 cloves garlic, minced
1 cup beef broth
½ cup soy sauce
⅓ cup brown sugar
2 tablespoons cornstarch
4 tablespoons water

2 cups frozen broccoli florets
1 tablespoon sesame oil
White rice, cooked

Directions

1. Heat a wok over high heat. Add 2 tablespoons of oil, and fry the beef until browned. Drain it on paper towels.
2. Using the oil remaining in the wok (add about 1 tablespoon more, if needed), sauté the garlic until fragrant.
3. Add the broth, soy sauce, and sugar. Bring it to a boil.
4. Return the fried beef to the sauce. Let it simmer, covered, for about 10 minutes, until tender.
5. Scoop out about ¼ cup of the sauce from the wok and place in a small bowl.
6. Mix the cornstarch and water to make a slurry, and stir it into the wok.
7. Drop in broccoli and cook, stirring, for about 30 seconds to thicken the sauce and heat through.
8. Drizzle with sesame oil and serve hot over rice.

Chicken and Duck Recipes

Empress Chicken

Serves: 4
Preparation Time: 5 minutes plus 30 minutes marinating time
Cooking Time: 15 minutes

Ingredients
<u>For marinade</u>
2 tablespoons cornstarch
1 tablespoon soy sauce

For sauce

1 tablespoon rice wine
2 tablespoons soy sauce
1 tablespoon sugar
1 teaspoon salt
1 teaspoon cornstarch
1 teaspoon sesame oil

1 pound boneless chicken, chopped into 1-inch pieces
1 cup cooking oil
10 dried hot red peppers or according to taste
1 teaspoon Sichuan peppercorns (Chinese coriander)
1 teaspoon ginger, minced
4 cups rice for serving

Directions

1. Mix the chicken, cornstarch, and soy sauce in a bowl. Let it marinate for 30 minutes.
2. Combine the ingredients for the sauce and set it aside.
3. When the chicken is ready, heat a wok over high heat. Add the oil and fry the marinated chicken until browned. Use a slotted spoon or spider strainer to remove it to a cooling rack or paper towels.
4. Remove any oil from the wok in excess of 2 tablespoons.
5. Sauté the dried peppers and Sichuan peppercorns for about 30 seconds.
6. Return the pre-fried chicken to the wok. Add the ginger and stir-fry for 1 minute.
7. Stir in the sauce and cook until thickened.
8. Serve hot, with rice.

Lemon Chicken

Serves: 12
Preparation Time: 5 minutes plus 15 minutes marinating time
Cooking Time: 30 minutes

Ingredients
3 pounds chicken breast fillets, halved

For marinade
1 tablespoon rice wine
1 tablespoon soy sauce
½ teaspoon salt

For batter
2 large eggs, beaten
¼ cup cornstarch
½ teaspoon baking powder

<u>Other ingredients</u>
2 cups vegetable oil, for frying
2 tablespoons vegetable oil
1 lemon, sliced
1 cup chicken broth
1/3 cup sugar
1 tablespoon cornstarch
1 tablespoon lemon juice
1 teaspoon salt

Directions

1. Combine the ingredients for the marinade, and marinate the chicken for 15 minutes.
2. When the chicken is ready, mix together the ingredients for the batter. Dip the chicken in the batter, coating each piece well.
3. Heat a wok over high heat and add the oil for frying. Reduce the heat to medium high, and fry the chicken until it is golden in color. Remove it and drain over paper towels.
4. Cut the chicken into bite-size pieces and arrange them on a serving dish.
5. In a non-stick frying pan, heat 2 tablespoons oil and stir-fry the lemon slices over medium heat.
6. Quickly mix the remaining chicken broth, sugar, cornstarch, lemon juice, and salt in a small bowl and pour it over the lemon slices.
7. Cook for 3 minutes more, or until sauce is thickened and translucent.
8. Pour the sauce over the chicken and serve hot.

Moo Goo Gai Pan Recipe

Serves: 3
Preparation Time: 30 Minutes
Cooking Time: 15 Minutes

Ingredients
10 ounces chicken breast fillet, cut into thin slices
⅓ cup vegetable or peanut oil

For marinade
1 egg white, lightly beaten
⅛ teaspoon ground white pepper
½ teaspoon salt

For sauce
¼ cup chicken broth
1 tablespoon light soy sauce
¼ teaspoon sesame oil
½ tablespoon sugar
3 dashes of ground white pepper
1 tablespoon rice wine
1 teaspoon cornstarch

Other ingredients
3 cloves garlic, peeled and minced
1 baby carrot, peeled and sliced thinly
½ of snow peas, trimmed
½ cup button mushrooms, sliced
½ cup straw mushrooms, sliced
½ teaspoon sugar
Salt to taste
Cooked rice, for serving

Directions
1. Combine the ingredients for the marinade. Mix well.
2. Marinate the chicken slices for about 10 minutes, making sure all are well-coated, and drain any excess marinade.
3. Heat a wok over high heat. Add the oil and heat up to almost the smoking point.
4. Stir-fry the chicken until it is half cooked (about 45 seconds).
5. Use a slotted spoon to remove the chicken from the wok and drain it on paper towels. Set it aside.
6. Transfer 2 tablespoons of the oil to a clean wok.
7. Stir-fry the garlic until it is slightly browned.
8. Add the carrot and snow peas and stir-fry for 2 minutes.

9. Add the mushrooms, and stir-fry for another 2 minutes.
10. Add the chicken and sauce ingredients. Stir well.
11. Cover and simmer until the chicken is well done and the sauce has thickened.
12. Add the sugar and salt to taste, and serve with rice.

Crispy Duck and Pancakes

Serves: 4
Preparation time: 20 minutes plus overnight salting
Cooking time: 1 ½ to 2 hours

Ingredients
4 whole duck legs

For overnight salting
1 teaspoon 5-spice powder
1 teaspoon Sichuan peppercorns, crushed
1 teaspoon salt

For baking
1 teaspoon honey
¾ cup chicken stock

For pancakes
2 cups flour, unsifted
¾ cup water

Sesame oil

<u>For serving</u>
Spring onions, julienned
Cucumber sticks
Hoisin sauce

Directions
1. Prick the duck legs all over using a fork or knife. Rub the salting ingredients into the duck legs. Let them sit, covered and refrigerated, overnight or for a few hours.
2. Preheat the oven to 400°F, and pat the duck legs dry with paper towels.
3. Place the duck legs face down in a non-stick frying pan.
4. Cook over high heat, not turning, until the skin begins to become crisp and brown (about 5 minutes). Flip them over and brown the other side as well.
5. Arrange the browned duck legs in a baking pan or oven-proof dish.
6. Drizzle them with honey and pour in the chicken stock.
7. Bake for 20 minutes, and then reduce the oven temperature to 275°F and bake for 1 hour. The duck flesh should fall off the bone at this point.
8. While the duck legs are in the oven, prepare the pancake dough. (See below)
9. When the duck legs are ready, remove them from the oven and let them cool for a short while.
10. Shred the duck meat with 2 forks, sprinkle it with spring onion, and serve it with hot pancakes, cucumber, and hoisin sauce.

To make pancakes

1. Boil the water.
2. Place the flour in a bowl and make a well in the center.
3. Add the hot water and mix. You may gradually add more flour to get a kneadable dough.
4. Knead the dough on a floured surface for 5 minutes, then cover and let it rest for 30 minutes.
5. Knead it again for 5 minutes, and roll it into a 1 ½-inch cylinder.
6. Divide the cylinder into 16 pieces, and roll each piece into a smooth ball.
7. Spread some sesame oil on your hands and flatten a ball of dough.
8. Roll it into a smooth disc, and brush the top with sesame oil. Make another disc of a similar size and place on top of first disc. Roll them out into a 6- to7-inch diameter double disc. Repeat for the rest of the dough balls.
9. Heat a skillet until water sprinkled into it bounces about in a small balls. Brush on a thin coat of sesame oil. Cook the double pancakes for 30 seconds on each side, without any browning. Remove them from the pan and slap them on a hard surface to separate the 2 discs. Peel away the 2 discs from each other, and place them on a sheet of foil. Repeat this procedure for the rest of the discs.
10. To steam the pancakes, form a packet by sealing foil over the discs. Place the foil packet in a steamer or double boiler and steam it for 20-30 minutes.

Sesame Chicken

Serves: 4
Preparation Time: 10-15 minutes
Cooking Time: 15 minutes

Ingredients
6 skinless chicken fillets, halved
2 tablespoons sesame seeds

For basting
2 tablespoons lemon juice
2 tablespoons soy sauce
¼ cup ketchup
1 tablespoon sesame oil
¼ teaspoon ground ginger
2 teaspoons brown sugar

Directions

1. Preheat a grill to medium-high heat, and pat chicken dry with paper towels.
2. Combine ingredients for basting.
3. Grill the chicken for 10-13 minutes, turning the chicken over and brushing or basting frequently with the mixture.
4. The chicken is done when there is no longer any trace of pink and the juices run clear.
5. Remove the chicken from the grill and sprinkle with it sesame seeds before serving.

Kung Pao Chicken Recipe

Serves: 3-4
Preparation Time: 15 minutes
Cooking Time: 10 minutes

Ingredients
<u>For marinade</u>
2 teaspoons soy sauce
2 teaspoons Chinese rice wine
2 teaspoons cornstarch
1 teaspoon Sichuan peppercorns

<u>For sauce</u>
1 tablespoon Chinese black vinegar
1 tablespoon chicken stock
3 teaspoons sugar
2-3 teaspoons soy sauce
2 teaspoons cornstarch
1/2 teaspoon sesame oil

Other ingredients
1 pound skinless boneless chicken breasts, cut into 1/2 -
inch cubes
1 tablespoon peanut or vegetable oil
8 dried red chilies, split length wise and seeds removed
1 teaspoon Sichuan peppercorns
4 garlic cloves, minced
1 tablespoon fresh ginger, minced
3 scallions, white parts thinly sliced, green parts set
aside cut into 1-inch strips
⅓ cup unsalted dry-roasted peanuts

Directions

1. Whisk the ingredients for the marinade together, and marinade the chicken for 20 minutes.
2. Whisk the sauce ingredients together, and set aside.
3. Heat a wok over high heat until almost smoking. Add the oil.
4. Turn off the heat and add the red peppers and the Sichuan peppercorns. Cook, while stirring, for 1 minute. Make sure the chilies do not get burned.
5. Turn the heat back on, and set it to medium-high.
6. Add the marinated chicken, and stir-fry until the chicken is half cooked.
7. Stir in the garlic and ginger, and cook for about 2 more minutes.
8. Gradually add the sauce, one tablespoon at a time. Allow the chicken to absorb the flavors while cooking.
9. When the chicken is done, add the green onion and peanuts.
10. Serve hot.

General Tso's Chicken

Serves: 4
Preparation Time: 1 hour 15 minutes
Cooking Time: 10 minutes

Ingredients
4 pieces chicken fillet, cut into 1-inch pieces

For the marinade and sauce
½ cup hoisin sauce
¼ cup white vinegar
3 tablespoons soy sauce
3 tablespoons sugar
2 tablespoons cornstarch
1 ½ cups water

For sautéing
1 tablespoon vegetable oil
4 garlic cloves, minced
2 tablespoons grated fresh ginger

½ teaspoon red pepper flakes, crushed

For coating and deep frying
3 egg whites
1 ½ cups cornstarch
½ cup all-purpose flour
½ teaspoon baking soda
4 cups vegetable oil

For garnish
2 green onions, chopped

Directions
1. Combine the ingredients for the marinade in a bowl. Separate ⅓ cup of the marinade and use it to marinate the chicken for 30 minutes, refrigerated. Set aside the remaining, for sauce.
2. Heat a wok over high and heat the oil. Reduce the heat to medium-high, and add the garlic, ginger, and pepper flakes. Sauté until fragrant.
3. Stir in the remaining sauce mixture (about 2 cups) and cook, stirring constantly, until thickened. Remove it from the heat and cover. Keep it warm.
4. In a bowl, whisk the egg whites until frothy. In a separate bowl, combine the rest of the ingredients for the coating, and mix until the consistency is similar to coarse meal.
5. Drain the marinated chicken and pat it dry with paper towels. Dip each piece in the egg whites, and then coat with the cornstarch mixture.
6. Fry the chicken at 350°F until it is golden brown (about 3 minutes). Drain on paper towels.
7. Reheat the sauce to a simmer. Add the chicken and stir to coat.
8. Serve.

Orange Chicken and Vegetable Stir-Fry

Serves: 4-6
Preparation Time: 15 minutes
Cooking Time: 10 minutes

Ingredients

For sauce

½ cup orange juice
2 tablespoons soy sauce
2 tablespoons rice vinegar
1 tablespoon oyster sauce
1 tablespoon orange zest
2 cloves garlic
1 teaspoon ginger, peeled and minced
1 ½ teaspoons honey, or to taste

For stir-fry

1 pound chicken tenderloin, cut into bite-size pieces
Salt and pepper
3 tablespoons cornstarch

1 cup chopped broccoli, sliced
1 cup carrots, sliced
1 cup snow peas, trimmed
½ cup celery, sliced
½ cup mushrooms, sliced
2-3 tablespoons peanut or vegetable oil
½ cup medium yellow onion, chopped
Rice, for serving

Directions

1. Place all the sauce ingredients in a blender and blend for 10-15 seconds.
2. Transfer to a saucepan, and heat to a simmer. Cook for 5 minutes.
3. Pat the chicken dry with paper towels.
4. Mix together the salt, pepper, and cornstarch, and coat the chicken with the mixture.
5. In a saucepan or wok, boil enough water to cover the vegetables. Drop the broccoli, carrots, snow peas and mushrooms in the boiling water, and simmer for 3-5 minutes. Remove the vegetables from the water and drain on paper towels.
6. Heat a clean wok over medium high heat. Add the peanut oil and fry the onions with the chicken for 3-5 minutes.
7. Add the pre-boiled vegetables, and stir-fry for 2 minutes.
8. Gradually add the sauce while stirring constantly, allowing a few seconds between additions. The sauce should thicken and coat chicken pieces.
9. Serve while hot over rice.

Fish and Seafood Recipes

Shrimp with Lobster Sauce

Serves: 2
Preparation Time: 10 minutes
Cooking Time: 10 minutes

Ingredients
2 cups water
4 ounces ground pork
2 tablespoons vegetable oil
1 clove garlic, minced
10 shrimps, peeled and deveined
1 tablespoon rice wine
1 ½ cups chicken or seafood stock
½ teaspoon sesame oil
¼ teaspoon sugar
½ teaspoon salt
Ground white pepper, to taste
½ cup frozen peas

1 small carrot, diced
2 tablespoons cornstarch
2 tablespoons water
1 egg, beaten slightly
1 green onion, chopped for garnish

Directions
1. Boil the water in a wok or pan. Add the pork and boil for 1 minute, breaking up any lumps. When the pork is no longer pink, drain it in a strainer and rinse it quickly.
2. Dry the wok and heat it over medium heat. Add the oil and sauté the garlic until fragrant. Add the pork and shrimp, and stir-fry for 20 seconds.
3. Add the wine and cook for 10 seconds more.
4. Stir in the chicken stock, sesame oil, sugar, salt, white pepper, peas and diced carrots.
5. Bring the mixture to a simmer.
6. In a bowl, stir cornstarch and water together to make a slurry. Pour this into the wok.
7. Allow it to cook and thicken enough to coat a spoon. If it gets too thick, it can be thinned with water.
8. Pour the slightly beaten egg over the wok and allow it to simmer for 5 seconds.
9. Fold the egg over slightly with a spatula.
10. Serve hot over rice. Sprinkle with green onions.

Salt and Pepper Squid

Serves: 4
Preparation Time: 10 minutes
Cooking Time: 7-10 minutes

Ingredients

1 ½ pounds squid, washed, cleaned, cut in uniform bite-size pieces
1 tablespoon rice wine
½ teaspoon sesame oil
Cooking oil for deep-frying
½ cup all-purpose flour
½ cup semolina flour
⅓ cup plain cornmeal
1 teaspoon salt, or to taste
White pepper, to taste, preferably freshly-cracked
1 tablespoon cooking or peanut oil or stir-frying
2 teaspoons ginger, minced
5 cloves garlic, sliced
2 long hot green peppers, cut lengthwise and thinly sliced

Cooked rice, for serving

Directions
1. Drain and dry the cleaned, cut squid with paper towels.
2. Combine the wine and sesame oil in a bowl. Marinate the squid for about 5 minutes.
3. Heat the oil for deep frying to 325°F in a wok or pot. The oil should be about 4 inches deep.
4. In a bowl, combine all-purpose flour, semolina flour, cornmeal, salt, and white pepper, and set aside.
5. When the oil is at the right temperature, gently squeeze the liquid from the squid and dredge it in the flour mixture.
6. Use a spider strainer or long handled sieve to lower the squid into oil, and fry until golden brown, 2-3 minutes.
7. Drain the squid on a plate lined with paper towels, and sprinkle with more white pepper.
8. Heat a clean wok over high heat. Add the tablespoon of oil and ginger. Cook until fragrant.
9. Stir in the garlic, and cook until lightly golden.
10. Add the peppers and stir-fry 30 seconds more.
11. Stir in the squid to heat through and to absorb the flavors, about 1 minute.
12. Serve hot over rice.

Kung Pao Shrimps

Serves: 2
Preparation Time: 10 minutes
Cooking Time: 5 minutes

Ingredients
1 pound medium shrimps, peeled and deveined

For marinade
1 tablespoon rice wine
1 teaspoon cornstarch
½ teaspoon salt

For sauce
1 tablespoon sugar
2 tablespoons water
1 tablespoon Chinese black vinegar
1 tablespoon soy sauce
¾ teaspoon cornstarch
½ teaspoon sesame oil

<u>Other ingredients</u>
2 tablespoons vegetable oil
1 large green or red bell pepper, seeds removed and thinly sliced
1 tablespoon garlic, minced
1 tablespoon ginger, peeled and minced
3 Thai chilies, broken in half and seeded
¼ cup chopped unsalted, dry-roasted peanuts
3 cups cooked rice

Directions

1. Stir the marinade ingredients together, and marinate the shrimps for 10 minutes.
2. Whisk together the ingredients for the sauce. Set aside.
3. Heat a wok over high heat, and swirl in the oil.
4. Add the bell pepper, garlic, ginger, and chilies, and stir-fry for 1 minute.
5. Add the shrimps, and stir-fry for 2 minutes or until the shrimps have turned orange.
6. Stir in the sauce, and cook until thickened, about 30 seconds.
7. Sprinkle with peanuts and serve over rice.

Fish with Black Bean Sauce

Serves: 4
Preparation Time: 5 minutes
Cooking Time: 15 minutes

Ingredients

<u>For the sauce</u>
4 tablespoons black bean sauce
1 teaspoon ginger, minced
2 teaspoons garlic powder
3 tablespoons rice wine
1 teaspoon toasted sesame oil
2 tablespoons white sugar

<u>Other ingredients</u>
4 pounds fish fillets, towel dried and cut into bite-sized pieces
1 tablespoon cornstarch
5 tablespoons cooking or vegetable oil, divided
1 medium onion, chopped

1 large green bell pepper, seeded and chopped
1 large red bell pepper, seeded and chopped
3 cloves garlic, minced
3 dried red chilies (optional)
Cooked rice, for serving

Directions
1. Whisk the sauce ingredients together in a bowl. Set aside.
2. Coat the fish with the cornstarch, and set aside.
3. Heat a wok over high heat. Swirl in the oil and add the onion, bell peppers, garlic and chilies (optional). Stir to combine.
4. Add ⅓ cup of sauce mixture to the wok, and continue cooking until the vegetables are tender. Using a slotted spoon, transfer the mixture to a plate, and set aside.
5. Using the same wok, add 3 tablespoons oil. Add the fish, and stir.
6. Pour in remaining the sauce mixture and continue cooking until the fish turns opaque.
7. Return the vegetables to the wok. Continue cooking and stirring until everything is heated through.
8. Serve with rice.

Shanghai Shrimp Stir-fry

Serves: 4
Preparation Time: 15 minutes
Cooking Time: 10 minutes

Ingredients

1 pound medium shrimp, shelled, deveined, washed, and drained
1 cup oil, for frying
2 green onions, white portion only
3 slices ginger
1 tablespoon rice wine
½ cup chicken broth
1 teaspoon sugar
¼ teaspoon Chinese black vinegar
1 teaspoon sesame oil
Salt, to taste

Directions

1. Pat the shrimps dry with paper towels.
2. Heat a wok over high heat. Add the oil and fry the shrimps for about 10 seconds, or until opaque. Fry in batches so as not to crowd the shrimps in the wok. You may use a spider strainer to lower and lift the shrimps, as well as while draining the oil back into the wok. Set them aside.
3. Heat the oil in the wok almost to the smoking point. Lower the shrimp once again into the oil and fry for 5-10 seconds. Frying too long will cause shrimps to be dry. Remove them from the wok and turn off the heat.
4. Carefully remove all oil in excess of 1 tablespoon, and reheat the oil over low heat.

5. Sauté the green onion whites and ginger until fragrant.
6. Add the wine, broth, sugar, and vinegar. Bring to a simmer and stir for 30 seconds.
7. Return the shrimp to the wok and add the sesame oil. Stir-fry for 5-10 seconds, just to coat the shrimp with sauce.
8. Season with salt to taste, and serve.

Cashew Shrimp Stir-fry

Serves: 4
Preparation Time: 30 minutes plus 2 hours marinating time
Cooking Time: 5 minutes

Ingredients
8 ounces medium shrimp, peeled and deveined

For soaking
1 teaspoon sugar
⅛ teaspoon baking soda
¼ cup water

For marinade
½ teaspoon sesame oil
1 teaspoon cornstarch
Salt and white pepper

For blanching
Water, for boiling
4 stalks celery, cut into bite-sized pieces diagonally
1 small bell pepper, diced
Ice water

For stir-fry
1 ½ tablespoons vegetable or peanut oil
2 slices ginger, minced
1 green onion, chopped
¼ teaspoon sugar
2 teaspoons oyster sauce
¾ cup roasted cashews
Salt and pepper

Directions

1. Combine the ingredients for soaking, and immerse the shrimps. Cover and refrigerate for 2 hours.
2. Remove from refrigerator, drain and rinse well with cold water. Drain, and pat dry with paper towels.
3. Mix the ingredients for the marinade together. Add the shrimp, and set aside.
4. Boil just enough water to cover the celery and bell pepper in a pot. Blanch the vegetables by immersing them in boiling water for just 30 seconds. Lift them out of the water and quickly immerse them in ice water. Drain, and set aside.
5. Heat a wok over medium heat. Swirl in the oil and add the ginger and green onion. Stir-fry for 1 minute.
6. Turn the heat up to high and add the shrimps.
7. When the shrimps turn pink, add the blanched vegetables.
8. Mix in the sugar, oyster sauce, and cashews, and cook just to heat through.
9. Season with salt and pepper, according to taste.

Fish with Spicy Bean Sauce

Serves: 4
Preparation Time: 20 minutes
Cooking Time: 15 minutes

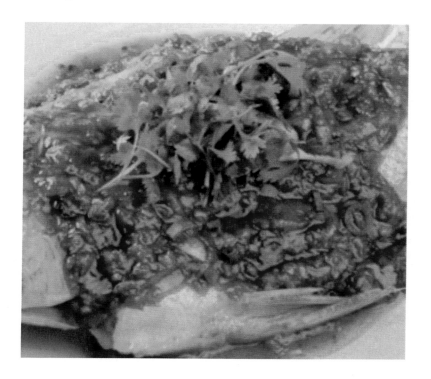

Ingredients
1 large tilapia fillet

For slurry
1 tablespoon water
1 tablespoon cornstarch

For sauce
1 tablespoon rice wine
1 tablespoon spicy bean sauce (douban)
1 teaspoon hoisin sauce

½ teaspoon sesame oil
½ teaspoon sugar
Ground white pepper

Other ingredients
1-2 tablespoons vegetable or peanut oil, or as needed
1 clove garlic, minced
¼ cup finely chopped onion
¼ cup ground pork
¼ cup shiitake mushrooms, finely chopped
¼ cup carrot, finely chopped
¼ cup finely chopped red pepper
½ cup water
1 teaspoon sesame oil
Cooked rice, for serving

For garnish
2 teaspoons cilantro, chopped
2 teaspoons green onion, chopped

Directions
1. Use a steamer, or steam the fish on a heatproof plate on a rack over 1 inch of water, covered, for 10 minutes. The fish is done when a butter knife can easily cut through it to the bottom. Remove it from the heat and place it on a serving dish.
2. Combine the ingredients for the slurry in a small bowl, and set aside.
3. Mix the ingredients for the sauce together, and set aside.
4. Heat a wok over high heat. Add the oil with the onions and garlic, and cook for a few seconds until fragrant.
5. Add the pork, mushrooms, carrot, and bell pepper. Stir-fry for about 1 minute.

6. Stir in the sauce and water, and bring it to a simmer.
7. Stir in the slurry and cook until the sauce coats a spoon. Add water if sauce becomes too thick.
8. Season with the sesame oil, remove it from the heat, and pour it over the steamed fish.
9. Sprinkle with cilantro and green onion, and serve hot over rice.

Vegetarian Recipes

Mixed Vegetables

Serves: 2
Preparation time: 10 minutes
Cooking time: 8 minutes

Ingredients
For thickener (slurry)
2 ½ teaspoons cornstarch
1 tablespoon water

For stir-fry
1 tablespoon vegetable oil
1 clove garlic, minced
1 small red pepper, sliced
1 small carrot, sliced
4 mushrooms, sliced
½ cup bamboo shoots

½ cup water chestnuts
1 cup broccoli florets
½ cup vegetable stock
Salt, to taste
2 teaspoons soy sauce

Directions
1. Combine the ingredients for the thickener and stir. Set aside.
2. Heat the oil in a wok over high heat. Add the garlic, and stir-fry until fragrant.
3. Add the red bell pepper, carrots, mushrooms, bamboo shoots, and water chestnuts. Stir-fry for 1 minute.
4. Add the bean sprouts and stir-fry for 2 minutes.
5. Pour in the vegetable stock, and bring it to a boil.
6. Give the thickener a quick stir before pouring it into the wok. Stir until it thickens.
7. Add the salt, soy sauce, and adjust according to your taste.
8. Serve while hot.

Dry-Sautéed Green Beans

Serves: 4
Preparation Time: 5 minutes
Cooking Time: 10 minutes

Ingredients

2 tablespoons peanut oil for stir-frying, or as needed
1 pound Chinese long beans, trimmed and cut into 3-inch pieces
1 tablespoon garlic, chopped
1 tablespoon ginger, chopped
2 green onions, white parts only, finely chopped
½ teaspoon chili paste
1 tablespoon dark soy sauce
½ teaspoon sugar
Salt and pepper, to taste
Sesame seeds for garnish

Directions

1. Heat a wok over medium heat. Swirl in 1 tablespoon of oil.
2. Add the beans and stir-fry until they shrivel and become slightly browned, about 7 minutes, then remove them to drain on paper towels. Set aside.
3. Adjust the heat to high, and add another tablespoon of oil.
4. Sauté the garlic, ginger, and green onions until fragrant.
5. Add the chili paste and stir to release the aroma.
6. Return the beans to the wok, and stir in the soy sauce, sugar, salt, and pepper.
7. Stir and adjust seasonings according to taste.
8. Sprinkle with sesame seeds and serve immediately.

Salt and Pepper Tofu

Serves: 2-4
Preparation Time: 10 minutes
Cooking Time: 10 minutes

Ingredients
For tofu
1 14-ounce block extra firm tofu, drained
4 tablespoons corn starch
Salt and pepper
Vegetable or peanut oil for frying

For stir-fry
1 tablespoon vegetable or peanut oil
1 cup leeks, white parts only, chopped
½ cup celery, chopped
½ cup green pepper, chopped
1 tablespoon garlic, minced
1 tablespoon ginger, minced
1 tablespoon light soy sauce
½ teaspoon brown sugar

<u>For garnish</u>
Green onions, chopped
Chili sauce

Directions

1. Combine the cornstarch, salt and pepper in a medium bowl.
2. Pat the tofu dry with paper towels, and cut it into cubes.
3. Toss the tofu cubes in the cornstarch mixture, making sure to coat each cube thoroughly.
4. Heat a wok over high heat. Add oil up to ½-inch deep, and allow it to heat up.
5. Fry the cubes in batches; do not crowd the wok, or the tofu will not be crispy. Flip to ensure all sides are golden brown.
6. Drain the tofu on paper towels.
7. Heat a clean wok over medium-high heat. Swirl in 1 tablespoon of oil, and stir-fry the leeks, celery, and green pepper for 2 minutes.
8. Add the ginger and garlic, and stir-fry 2 minutes longer.
9. Stir in the soy sauce and brown sugar, and cook for about 30 seconds more, then add the tofu cubes and toss well.
10. Garnish with green onions and serve with chili sauce on the side.

Mapo Tofu

Serves: 3-4
Preparation Time: 5 minutes
Cooking Time: 15 minutes

Ingredients
<u>For thickener</u>
½ cup chicken or vegetable broth
1 teaspoon cornstarch
2 teaspoons soy sauce
1 teaspoon sugar

<u>For stir-fry</u>
1 tablespoon sesame oil
2 cloves garlic, minced
2 teaspoons ginger, minced
4 green onions, white part only, minced
1 tablespoon fermented black beans, roughly chopped
½ teaspoon Sichuan peppercorns, black seeds removed, ground

6 ounces vegetarian ground meat substitute*
2 teaspoons chili bean paste
1 14-ounce block silken tofu, drained and cut into ¾-inch cubes

For garnish
Green onions, green part only, minced

Directions
1. In a bowl, mix together the ingredients for the thickener. Set aside.
2. Heat the sesame oil in a wok over high heat. Stir-fry the garlic, ginger, and green onions until fragrant.
3. Add the black beans and Sichuan pepper. Stir for a few seconds.
4. Add the ground pork and break up any lumps while stirring. Cook until the pork is browned.
5. Stir in chili bean paste, mixing well.
6. Add the tofu pieces and toss, being careful not to mash them.
7. Stir the thickener, and pour it into the wok.
8. Stir the contents of the wok, and bring the sauce to a boil. When the sauce is thickened, remove the wok from the heat.
9. Garnish with green onion and serve with rice.

* For non-vegetarian, you can use ground pork.

Egg Foo Yung

Serves: 4
Preparation Time: 30 minutes
Cooking Time: 20 minutes

Ingredients
3 tablespoons peanut oil, or as needed
Rice for serving

For omelet
6 eggs, beaten
1 cup bean sprouts
¼ cup green onions, minced
¼ cup Chinese cabbage, shredded
4 water chestnuts, minced
½ cup ground vegetarian meat substitute or tofu, chopped
1 teaspoon soy sauce

For thickener
1 tablespoon cornstarch
2 tablespoons water

For Sauce
1 cup vegetable broth
1 tablespoon soy sauce
2 teaspoons sugar
2 teaspoons vinegar

Rice for serving

Directions
1. In a bowl, combine the ingredients for the omelet. Mix well.
2. Heat a wok over moderate heat. Swirl in the oil.
3. Scoop out about ⅓ cup of the egg mixture, and spread it in a circular motion into the wok.
4. When bottom is browned, flip it over to brown other side. Transfer it to a plate.
5. Stir the egg mixture, and scoop to make another omelet. Repeat until the omelet mixture is used up.
6. Combine the cornstarch and water to make thickener.

7. Mix the ingredients for the sauce in a saucepan. Bring it to a boil and simmer.
8. Stir in the thickener, and simmer until it is thick enough to coat a spoon.
9. Serve with omelet (egg foo young). The sauce may be poured over the omelet, or served in a separate bowl. Place omelet over rice for serving.

Dessert Recipes

Fortune Cookies

Serves: 36
Preparation Time: 15 minutes
Cooking Time: 10 minutes

Ingredients
3 egg whites
¾ cup white sugar
½ cup butter, melted and cooled
¼ teaspoon vanilla extract
¼ teaspoon almond extract
1 cup all-purpose flour
2 tablespoons water

Directions

1. Prepare fortunes on strips of paper.
2. Preheat the oven to 375°F.
3. Line cookie sheets with parchment paper, or spray with non-stick spray.
4. Using an electric mixer, whip the egg whites and sugar at high speed until frothy, about 2 minutes.
5. Reduce the mixer speed to low, and mix in the melted butter, vanilla, almond extract, flour, and water.
6. Spoon the batter onto the cookie sheets in 3-inch circles. Repeat until the batter is used up. Be sure to leave enough space between circles.
7. Bake until the edges begin to turn golden brown, 5-7 minutes. Do not overbake, or they will be too stiff to fold. If you under-bake them, their texture will be too spongy.
8. Quickly take a circle, put the fortune strip on the center, and fold the cookie in half over the fortune.
9. Fold the ends together to make a horseshoe shape.
10. Allow to cool and set. You may put them in muffin pans to prevent them from springing open.

Mango Pudding

Serves: 8
Preparation Time: 3 hours setting time
Cooking Time: 15 minutes

Ingredients

2 tablespoons/envelopes unflavored gelatin
¾ cup sugar
1 cup hot water
3 cups fresh mangoes, pureed
1 cup evaporated milk
8 ice cubes
Whipped cream and fresh mango slices or cubes for garnish

Directions

1. Dissolve the gelatin and sugar in hot water. Make sure there are no lumps or undissolved gelatin.
2. Combine the mango puree, evaporated milk, and ice cubes in a large bowl.
3. Pour the mango mixture into the gelatin mixture while stirring. Continue stirring until the ice cubes are melted.
4. Pour into molds and chill to set (about 3 hours).
5. When set, loosen the edges with a butter knife and invert the mold over a serving dish. You can also briefly dip the mold into hot water to loosen.
6. Garnish with whipped cream and mango slices.

Conclusion

Chinese takeout is an important part of American history and culture. Cooking the dishes in this book is a participation in America's cultural heritage. Although you won't enjoy the convenience of simply having it delivered to your doorstep, making your own Chinese takeout-inspired dishes will be a unique experience as well as an opportunity to prepare healthy food for yourself and your family.

Enjoy the adventure!

Appendix - Cooking Conversion Charts

1. Volumes

US Fluid Oz.	US	US Dry Oz.	Metric Liquid ml
¼ oz.	2 tsp.	1 oz.	10 ml.
½ oz.	1 tbsp.	2 oz.	15 ml.
1 oz.	2 tbsp.	3 oz.	30 ml.
2 oz.	¼ cup	3½ oz.	60 ml.
4 oz.	½ cup	4 oz.	125 ml.
6 oz.	¾ cup	6 oz.	175 ml.
8 oz.	1 cup	8 oz.	250 ml.

Tsp.= teaspoon - tbsp.= tablespoon – oz.= ounce – ml.= millimeter

2. Oven Temperatures

Celsius (°C)	Fahrenheit (°F)
90	220
110	225
120	250
140	275
150	300
160	325
180	350
190	375
200	400
215	425
230	450
250	475
260	500

Made in the USA
Las Vegas, NV
07 February 2022

43364287R00083